Elder Tree

Elder Tree

Chris Ellery

LITERARY PRESS
LAMAR UNIVERSITY

ISBN: 978-1-942956-32-7
Library of Congress Control Number: 2016951395

Manufactured in the United States

Lamar University Literary Press
Beaumont, Texas

for Bill and Nobie

Poetry from Lamar University Literary Press

Bobby Aldridge, *An Affair of the Stilled Heart*
Michael Baldwin, *Lone Star Heart, Poems of a Life in Texas*
Charles Behlen, *Failing Heaven*
Alan Berecka, *With Our Baggage*
David Bowles, *Flower, Song, Dance: Aztec and Mayan Poetry*
Jerry Bradley, *Crownfeathers and Effigies*
Jerry Bradley and Ulf Kirchdorfer, editors, *The Great American Wise Ass Poetry Anthology*
Matthew Brennan, *One Life*
Paul Christensen, *The Jack of Diamonds is a Hard Card to Play*
Christopher Carmona, Rob Johnson, and Chuck Taylor, editors, *The Beatest State in the Union*
Chip Dameron, *Waiting for an Etcher*
William Virgil Davis, *The Bones Poems*
Jeffrey DeLotto, *Voices Writ in Sand*
Mimi Ferebee, *Wildfires and Atmospheric Memories*
Larry Griffin, *Cedar Plums*
Ken Hada, *Margaritas and Redfish*
Michelle Hartman, *Disenchanted and Disgruntled*
Michelle Hartman, *Irony and Irreverence*
Katherine Hoerth, *Goddess Wears Cowboy Boots*
Lynn Hoggard, *Motherland*
Gretchen Johnson, *A Trip Through Downer, Minnesota*
Ulf Kirchdorfer, *Chewing Green Leaves*
Laozi, *Daodejing*, tr. By David Breeden, Steven Schroeder, and Wally Swist
Janet McCann, *The Crone at the Casino*
Erin Murphy, *Ancilla*
Laurence Musgrove, *Local Bird*
Dave Oliphant, *The Pilgrimage, Selected Poems: 1962-2012*
Kornelijus Platelis, *Solitary Architectures*
Carol Coffee Reposa, *Underground Musicians*
Jan Seale, *The Parkinson Poems*
Steven Schroeder, *the moon, not the finger, pointing*
Carol Smallwood, *Water, Earth, Air, Fire, and Picket Fences*
Glen Sorestad *Hazards of Eden*
W.K. Stratton, *Ranchero Ford/ Dying in Red Dirt Country*
Wally Swist, *Invocation*
Jonas Zdanys (ed.), *Pushing the Envelope, Epistolary Poems*
Jonas Zdanys, *Red Stones*

For information on these and other Lamar University Literary Press books go to
www.lamar.edu/literarypress

Acknowledgments

I am grateful to the editors of the following publications, where some of the poems in this collection originally appeared.

The Aurorean
AVOCET: A Journal of Nature Poems
Blue Hole
Cimarron Review
Crosstimbers
descant
The Enigmatist
Lifting the Sky: Southwestern Haiku & Haiga
New Texas
Sufi Journal
Texas Poetry Calendar

For the folklore and symbolism of the elder tree, my primary sources are www.thegoddesstree.com and Jane Gifford's *The Wisdom of Trees*.

I am indebted to my friend the late Mike McLean for first pointing out to me that one theory for the origin of the name "Ellery" is its connection with the elder tree, possibly with reference to the "island of the elder tree" or possibly as a phonetic corruption of the phrase "elder tree."

CONTENTS

At the Cottage Door

Rood Wood and Hanging Tree

The Triple Goddess

Berries and Brambles

The Thirteenth Moon

The lesson of the elder is a difficult one.
—Jane Gifford, *The Wisdom of Trees*

At the Cottage Door

At the Cottage Door

Under the eave at the cottage door
mystic elder shades and shapes
his going out, his coming in.

Like gentle hands of girlish spring
her flowers of milky pearl arouse
the first devotion of the child.

Quick as moonbeams on Midsummer Night
with green embrace she blesses love
with lightning heart and fairy luck.

In selfless reaping of ripening suns
her wine-sweet berries like drops of night
dye the blazing hair of autumn black.

Pluck a stick as you look inside
and plant it when the last full moon
calls your body to icy rest.

In winter dreams on Mother's breast
your pallid bones will root and grow
and leaf again as elder limbs.

Eager

new boy
listen
do you hear the dogs
they chase the feral hog
listen
their eager terror
dread
delight
that's what it means
to be a dog

boy
push your hand
into the dark
reach
for the crazy beast
tusk and bristle
the hot furious breath
feel
your heart
in the heart of that heat

Scarab

When the last of Daddy's many wrecks
broke an axle and his ankle, Mom swore
he'd never drive again. Therefore at night
she wrapped my brother and me like larvae in
our quilts and laid us, soggy with sleep, on the back
seat of our newest old machine to drive
our father to the Terminal. His job
was called the "Graveyard Shift." Our black Bel Air
lumbered through the dark deserted streets
like a half-ton scarab. In downtown shops
along the way the mute and elegant mannequins
grinned and waved at us from the Kingdom of
Unconsciousness. Eerie shadows entering
the windows tickled our laps. And when we stopped
on East Front Street, our sacred beetle raised
a wing and spat Dad out.

                         Now wide awake
we begged our mom to take us home the long
way back, across the spooky viaduct.
We knew that in the dark below the bridge
a scarecrow with a tow sack face and charcoal
eyes would watch us pass. The railings of
that dangerous span, showing their rust in the flash
of our brights, rattled like iron bones, the timbers
moaned, and our mother said, *One day this bridge
is bound to topple down and take us with it.*
My brother twined his goose-fleshed legs with mine
and brushing his crotch against my thigh revealed
his stiff, erotic dread. Why do we crave like sex
the terror of death? If I could ask, I'd ask
those rag-bound, mummified old kings long dead.

That afternoon, Mom turned us out to play
so she could watch the world turn on the edge
of night. While yellow pansies stared at us,

we boys exhumed by chance a rusty hatchet
from the flower bed. It was a sign.
To escape that ordinary summer day
we hacked the brick foundation of our house—
adventuresome fools desecrating tombs
in search of the mummies that came to life
on Saturdays in black & white inside
our RCA. The mortar all too easily
gave way. We scooped aside the rubble, crawled
into the crawl space underneath the house.

Cool and dry. The inner sanctum of
a pyramid. A little daylight filtered in
as if the house had eaten up the sun
and oozed a bit of it from up above.
In search of a gold sarcophagus we knocked
our heads on beams before discovering
that robbers had already robbed that tomb.
But not to let our raiding go to waste
we quickly cleared a space of spider webs
and in the dirt designed a labyrinth
of streets, complete with bridges built
of salvaged boards and metal scraps. We crashed
the tiny cars our father bought us every
payday at Burhman-Farr. He slept
in the room above us, and the weight of his dream
dripped down to the dust of our private necropolis.

A black dung beetle dropped from a piling.
It startled us, like the first curse.
Twitching frail antennae, it crawled toward us,
making hieroglyphic tracks in the dirt.
When it came to the bustling center
of our town, it parked there—dense star
of glistening blackness—like the heart of night,
beating with all the brightness of the universe.

Grimm House

Mr. Grimm's house overshadowed left field,
dirtiest corner of the vacant lot where our diamond lay—
snake hole, milkweed, chicken bones,
the dirty plate we used for home. We knew

the gargoyle tales of that drunken abode, the demon abuse
that bred inside to terrorize the neighborhood.
Against the savage derelict himself
I swung my bat—
                           the ball

as if it understood the base necessity of breaking glass,
like a flying rat, impossibly quick,
scurried through the air above the shaggy lot
toward one lazy eyelid of the leprous house.

Buckle and belt raised welts on my tenderest skin.
Three months' allowance went into the glazier's hand.
Still it thrills me to remember the physics of that swing
and the sweet, irrevocable splintering of the pane.

Premium

After warning Dad the premium is due
Mom goes to bed. The plates are in
the sink. The ice of her last drink
melting. She leaves the TV on
to save herself the effort of dreaming.
Alone at the kitchen table Dad signs
the check with a flourish, defiantly
thumbing his nose at the Redcoats.
Freeing the slaves. Endorsing his own
pardon—just a minute too late.
I happen to look away and see
the black elder tree in the moonlight
ripe with all the wisdom of the night.
When I look back again there's Dad
shoving his check in the envelope.
A secret love letter, papyrus scroll
of irresistible jazz. When he licks
the glue on the back of the flap
I savor the night-blue skin. My sweet
enemy, my forbidden queen.

Night Crawler

My father winced
when the night crawler tensed.
Wind wizened the face of the lake.

In water to their orange bellies,
our plastic bobbers
made a funny little *pas de deux*.

Dad got out the sandwiches he made
to get us through the afternoon.
The elder jelly soaked the bread.

As we ate, he said,
"Wouldn't this be good
with milk?"

He took me to a dairy once to see the rite
of getting it from udder to bottle.
A white river flowed

through a sheet metal trough
into the foaming mouth
of the pasteurizer.

We were fishermen now,
and no mothers were near.
His battle scar wriggled on his calf.

I was old before he told
me how it came to him
or why his shipmates called him "Shark."

Suddenly a fish was nibbling.
A thrill rose up in me from some deep trench.
"Wait, wait," he said. "Wait."

When I finally pulled my line from the water,
there was only the hook
with just a morsel of worm

still hugging the shank,
translucent
in the wholeness of the moment.

I Smell the Blood

Our neighbor's boy was also Jack, so I
was Little Jack and stuck to him like gum
to shoes. His buddies joked I needed sun,
for I was always in his shadow.

When Jack was Long John Silver, he named me
his Captain Flint and carried me upon
his shoulder, where I viewed more wickedness
than any devil. *Pieces of Eight! Pieces
of Eight! Blow me down! Ahoy me hearties!*
We took no prisoners, and slipped away
one glorious day with our African treasure.

Jack's hardball was the first to sting my mitt,
and when he swiped a six-pack of his father's
brew, I got a sip then slew STOP signs
with his .22 like giants. The highest branch
of the biggest oak was our F-4 Phantom. We flew
a thousand sorties over sea and land
before we crashed one leafy day in a wreck
of fractured limbs and splintered fuselage—
good thing us parrots mostly live forever.

Jack turned eighteen and joined the Marines.
He could not stay to build a house or trade
his mother's cow for beans, but quickly fell
three thousand miles to Vietnam and tripped,
un-nimbly, on a wire. *Semper fi.*
They put his pieces in a box
like Crackerjacks and flew it home to us
along with the American flag.

His mother couldn't bear to keep his collie.
I was glad. That dog was bred to be
a hero's helper, foe to giants.
Jack got her when he turned sixteen, and since

he loved the queen of Camelot with Courtly
Love he named that pup for her and said
she'd always be First Lady. In my yard
I lay with Jackie in the summer grass.
We looked to Jack's backyard and pined. First death
imprinted *carpe diem* on our minds
in Gothic letters. Thus our grief brought truant
days. We fished for pike or scared up coons
and armadillos in the darkest shade
of deepest woods. We found the Holy Grail
then rode out of the wilderness to teach
a kid what manhood is: A gun is just
as good or bad as the man, and since Jack Wilson
wasn't good, me and Jackie took a bullet
in the gut, but killed that low-down Yankee liar.
Yes, Jackie was a giant-slayer, trotting
beside my bike, growling at every Jack the Ripper.

When boyhood ripened on the stalk, I fumbled
my way through puberty with zits and passion,
practicing kisses with a feathery Jill,
my pillow. Jackie blinked her big brown eyes
in the night. I felt her furry heat nearby,
so I was fond of saying to my friends
that Jackie taught me how to love a bitch.
At the time I thought it sounded cool.
I was a fool pulling plums from pudding,
but it turned out true. Through rudderless years
she raised me from fathomless dark
to the heart's high wheel.

On the day we had to put her down,
I was reading a book by Kerouac. Japhy sprints
to the peak of the Matterhorn. Mist covers
the way to the clouds, where I know that I must go.
The giant that Jack never felled is waiting.
Grown old and gross in Desolation,
he is still sniffing the air for blood,

still guarding a treasure he cannot use or love.

Conjugation

Eight boys study Spanish in Taco Bell
El tiempo es malo.
Sí, esta sequía es terrible en Tejas.
(boys I call them)
ocho niños
from the nearby junior high
(seven are blond and one is brown)
all pouring sodas from the bottomless
                          fountain

Two girls come in
(girls I call them)
quiero quieres
     soy
     eres
     es
two raven-haired
Latinas (they are
                  from the nearby junior high)
and perch at a different table
indifferent to the
                gringo conjugations

A sudden sputter of rain
dresses the dusty parking lot
after months of drought
nueve meses
and a grackle (with golden eyes)
pecks
at the soggy corn of a fallen taco
warning his rivals
                with an eloquent squall

Across the Line in Le Flore County

Jim bought us beer
our last night in the tavern.

We were going back to school.
We would always be in school.

Monday morning
he'd be back to stocking shelves
in the Hatfield City Grocery.

He'd been in the Navy. Retired.
His uniform hangs in the closet
of the octagonal house he built himself
a hundred yards from the edge of Arkansas
a thousand miles from any place
anyone he ever knew would ever think
he might ever go.

From the road his house resembles
a big circus tent.
Round,
with shingled sides.

He told us the story,
how he pitched it there,
set by himself the tall center pole,
propped on his truck, backing up
until it dropped in the hole he had dug
one sweating afternoon,
making it plumb
with his tailgate and tamping bar.
His house will forever smell of creosote.

Why would he make an eight-sided house?

I can see that day,
the deep, straight hole.

Youth Dies in Rollover

Harper was no devotee of discipline.
He bore the scars of many accidents and fights,
chased the wild gods
into moonshine woods
and taverns where tattoos and taboos
were all the rage.
He wore black boots and skulls
on both his biceps. Often times

we wondered why we loved him.

He was quick to anger shooting pool,
as if the balls betrayed him.
His oaths were clumsy, comic and obscene,
and true. Sobriety brought
repentance and hard work
which he played at
with the same ferocity—
the planks and beams erected
by the sheer force of his hammer.
When he held a chainsaw
we stayed clear. Whacking at red oak, like sin,
he never paused
to calculate the line of fall
or holler timber.

No one was surprised
by when or how he died, mangled
among scraps of
                    steel, the
skulls
        of his biceps grinning in
a way that said

the world is now far less
a wonder
than it was.

Wintergreen Man

One summer, needing beans and fall
tuition, I took a job demolishing
a house, rust-roofed with rippled tin
and faded, century old at least, but square

and sturdy. Owner, name of Eoff,
had sold the lot to someone for
a fortune, subdivide or build a tavern
there for the rich kid college students.

He could have bull-dozed, burned, been done,
but wanted every bent and rusty nail,
every ply and plank and scrap that could
be salvaged. Old man lived there,

squatter I supposed, brittle and thorny
as dead, dry greenbrier. We called him
Wintergreen Man—the candy he kept
in his pockets and sometimes gave us.

He wouldn't leave that house even
when we pushed the corrugated roof
from over his head, pounding through
the attic. Crowbar and sledge

unwedged the quarter-sawed cherry wood.
The geezer raised his rabbits there. At first,
they hopped about, loose in the place,
dodging feet and falling boards.
                              Got-tamn it!

That's a twenty-dollar doe you nearly crushed!
On lunch breaks we could pet them.
The lumber smelled of sawmills, released
a dry, red screech as we cracked it, broke it

from the studs, surprised at the force
it took, sweat, grunts and iron leverage.
The wood held in the nails with the strength
of forests. The old man cussed us,

and we cussed him back—him, his temper,
and the rabbit shit that pellet by pellet
packed the tread of our boots—and moved
his junk and cages day by day to the yard

as level by level, room by room
we tore apart his home. One day he said
he'd take the chimney, wanted us to lay
it down, move it whole to the new place

he said he'd found, to draw the cold
when winter came, to keep his rabbits warm.
They munched in their cages in the shade
until the day the brick flue fell, crashing

into rubble. Bitter old man rage—the waste
of something made so well by hands that cared
for work, but all that we and all our kind
and *Got-tamn* age were good for was

to loiter, squander, devastate, and raze.
I couldn't say just where he went next day
with stuff and livestock, but near the end
of summer, he returned, as if he knew,

to see us pull the stripped frame down.
A skeleton of studs, still square
and sound, it took a half-ton truck
to winch it to the ground.

He told us how to do it, measured
the line of fall and showed us where
to hook our cable, around the hard wood beam
that bore the high oak trusses.

Rabbi Dizzle's Two Companions

Young Rabbi Dizzle, walking abroad, found on the street
a packet of jam, a condom, and a hypoderm.
Two hounds bounding from a bush playfully pursued.
One was black and one was white.

Young Rabbi Dizzle made a note: These things you see
enumerate, they are the world we have.
A right hand nail was split into the quick, and when
he stabbed it in his pocket, it caught on every thread.

Young Rabbi Dizzle tossed the needle, tossed the jam.
The two hounds went at last their ways.
He picked up the condom in its pristine pouch
and dropped it in his pants.

Tamales and Turquoise Trucks

Two buddies camped beside the water.
Zero fish. Zero nibbles.
Dead night crawlers and stinky shrimp.
Morning splurged in a lake's laugh.

In town we buy boots cigars rib-eyes.
We ask for tamales. The girl
at the deli in her red apron
chats us to her grandmother's house.

> *going north on the highway*
> *turn right at Fuller's Grocery*
> *a block and a half*
> *look for a turquoise truck*

Everybody in town loves those tamales.
We buy a dozen. Grandma,
short as a girl with great grinning choppers,
adds a couple extra.

All tamales should be made with such big love
by women with turquoise trucks.

First Farewell

I open the tackle box
you kept with your tools
on the oily shelf.
The last flies that you tied
pristine
in the little compartments.
Surely the trout in Mill Creek
have fretted about your absence.

Octopus

When I was just a young octopus, a young cephalopod,
young in the Indian Ocean, 8 were not enough, 8 arms
with all their suckers, all they could touch and grab, 1 foot
then 2 feet then 4 reaching longer, longer with every gulp
of plankton, every famished swallow of the larval stars,
8 feet then 16 reaching beyond my own eye into
the inky sea. Vessels went down around me. Sailors
fell around me swallowing prayers and screams.

Their gill-less breathing and wide-eyed writhing ceased,
and the wrecks fell past them as bodies relaxed to the sea,
turning and tossing with weightless agility, formless
and graceful, as though they had left their bones above.
I touched them all, touched their slow drift, gathered them
into myth as I loved their faces with eager tentacles,
loved them inside my pliant hood, loved them all with all
my three young hearts, with the love of a creature that dies

after mating, knowing their lips and eyes with the cups
of my boneless arms, knowing their vertebrate curves
with my skin, knowing their taste and temperature.
Alert for morays and sharks, I held them briefly, loving
their shapeless descent, the beauty of their rare gazes,
the flavor of their surprise. Then I released them young
to playful currents, substance itself their only propulsion,
eager and young to the teasing fingers of the deep.

Rood Wood and Hanging Tree

Golem

Inquisitive creature, lump of clay,
why do you stare at me
with such perplexity
through eyes of glass? You are not made
to know or ask, but to obey.

What arrogant powers from the gray,
wet earth brought you, brute,
stone-jawed, ignorant, and mute
of cunning words, you cannot say.
Clod, you cannot say.

Sleep, sleep the deepest sleep and wait.
Sleep and dream until
you are called by my will
to act. Then, as you are made
to live and serve a day,
sleep again, sleep in the cold clay.

Bomb

A mushroom shrouded my childhood,
sprouting one winter
from the 6 o-clock news.

I made mud pies in the ditch
where the rain drained into a culvert.
Such clean fun.

I remember the mockingbirds came
one by one to the birdbath.
Summer ripened the pear and plum.

Every fall in the blue above our house
the giant black jacks bloomed
with fire.

My mom kept an old kerosene lamp
in the closet and lit it
whenever lightning knocked the power out.

On Saturdays a quarter to dark
Mrs. Hooker burned
the hair she cut.

A circle scorched black on the ground
near the old chicken coop.
The chickens were gone.

Who knows what spells
she sent into the night with that smoke
to protect me?

A collie, my familiar, slept with her head
in my lap. I stroked her silky fur
and felt it burning.

Shooting Infinity
from the Bottom of Palo Duro Canyon

When last we used your old blue tent,
the one Sharon didn't want after the split,
you tried to photograph the stars, holding
the shutter button to the count of twelve,
time-lapse rotation of the Milky Way.

Back at the fire we laughed in our cups. You'd left
the focus set for close-up shots, a mere
five feet to shoot infinity from the bottom of
a canyon. You told how Sharon left
for no reason you could fathom,
a woman's heart remote as any galaxy.

Later, while we were sleeping off the beer,
an intruder in the camp disturbed us—
bandit-faced raccoon, big as a bear
in our flashlights (as we later swore to friends)
and unperturbed when we roused ourselves

to save the oatmeal cookies. Cold in the night air,
body heat lost from mummy bags, we shoved
supplies in the cab of the truck. You even locked
the doors and hid the keys—to be safe, you said,
imagining raccoons driving off with our cigarettes.

We woke to weak sun, stiff and swearing only fools
camp in the Canyon in January. The sound of horses
somewhere. We rubbed numbed fingers to build a fire.
Coffee drew our nearest neighbor several sites away.
A bearded lumberjack, alone. On his way

home to Wisconsin after weeks in Texas
selling Christmas trees, enough to tide him over,
so he said. We gave him hot black coffee

and bread, wished him happy homecoming
to his wife and child as he helped us fold the tent.

Since then we sleep in heated comfort when we camp,
braving winter for a so-called weekend out-of-doors.
Your trailer keeps our ice chest safe from coons.
And the beds are soft as befits the old men
we've become. Outside the window near my head

I watch the stars you tried to aim for light years
ago through a tiny aperture. I watch
so long I swear I see them spin around
the Pole. Like living flakes of light they seem and yet
not one inch closer than they were.

Suburb

Here in the night
of the crawling suburb,
powered by the amps
of its own construction,
one tower looms
above the others,
polished slab
with a hundred windows,
all lit but one.
Behind
that one black pane
that breaks the pattern
a man and woman
push wooden sticks
into rice
without looking:
the bare floor catches
a few soft grains.

Dear Jack

Who would have thought
the suburbs could ooze past Frisco
into my gut? Our saints fled New York,
the Dharma went disco.

The mortgage passed out in my lap
squeezing my bloated intestine.
In the Buckhorn I'm taking a nap
when the Hanged Man

pulls up the next stool,
sits, and orders a bourbon.
In this hell, spittle drenches the asphodel
and angels blow with abandon.

I'm juiceless, pour me another.
The bartender, man, is a turtle
descending on nobody's shoulder.
My buttons are the bones of my poodle.

Contemplative:
After Reading Stephen Crane

A flea on the hide of a mangy old hyena has a pretty limited view of things.

A flea on the hide of an old hyena has a rather narrow definition of reality.

For a certain flea, the horizon is the rump of a mangy old hyena.

A flea, not content with the curvature of the old hyena's back, conceived it to be a shadow cast on the wall of a cave.

A flea conceived a cave.

A certain discontented flea with too much time on his hands went searching for a premise on which to establish his own significance.

While a flea was thinking, his companion bit into the tasty flesh of the beast upon whose ass they were both residing.

Co-residence does not imply cohabitation.

The average flea lives about six weeks.

For every adult flea found on a hyena there are approximately ten fleas in various stages of development.

Existential reflection sets one flea apart from another.

Next thing you know the flea is writing philosophy. Or theology. Or a poem.

Next thing you know the flea is head writer for a hit sitcom.

Next thing you know the flea buys a Ferrari.

A hyena scratched and bit itself to no avail.

When the universe scratches and the whole world shakes, all a flea can do is just hang on.

A flea said to the Scavenger, "Sir, I exist."

Next thing you know the flea is promoting his latest self-help book.

A certain flea had a companion named Pete who took a certain delight in the fact that pleasure is the greatest good in life.

A flea said, "AUMMMM."

A restless mind is an empty belly.

Blessed is the flea that hungers and thirsts.

A flea, scorned and rejected by his tribe, wanting more, insisting on a truth greater than the flesh of a stinking scavenger, falls from the flesh of that rank beast into the muck of some steaming Ethiopian tributary.

Because the exoskeleton of a flea is shock resistant, a flea can survive a fall of five feet or more.

Once upon a time there was a certain flea who hadn't been seen to smile for many years. He dressed in scaly hyena skin and gobbled the air.

Next thing you know the flea is killing every flea that disagrees with him.

Under certain conditions, a flea can live as long as a year.

A flea got what he deserved.

Last thought of a certain flea as he fell from the scabby backside of a mangy old hyena: *Transcendence!*

A certain flea died alone.

It was only a flea.

Venus and Mars

In dreams, the blind man sees
the bones of comrades in muddy light.
I was born under a soggy sky
the day my father died in Vietnam.

In dreams, the blind man feels
his lover's hands on his hair.
Never did eyes of a mouse wish more
for the owl—if only her wings were real.

But Venus crosses in front of the sun,
forced to witness every murder. Killing,
killing—the goddess with the key
can't find the lock. Blood unstinting.

We know fixed stars aren't really fixed.
We know the planets aren't really stars.
Dogwoods bloom and jonquils line the roads
where I pass in dreams to love and war.

Cardinal

Somewhere summer has surely startled virginity
from a thousand brides. If not virginity, then maidenhood,
to speak in my old-fashioned way
in these unsentimental times.
But here, in my back yard,
among the squirrels frolicking in the live oak,
the lizards and the rats romping on my fence—yes, rats—
I've seen many female cardinals, demur coloration,
but not one male.
        I've watched for them
in evenings, voyeur-like with six-packs and cigarettes,
more Buddha than Marlboro Man (don't think I haven't),
watched and listened, big-bellied and repressed,
for their flirtatious twittering.
Their ostentatious charm has left summer at the altar.

Perhaps they've gone out frisking one another,
all-masculine dance of plumage.
Perhaps they've sworn an oath, sensing Armageddon.
May be they've gone to Canada to dodge
the draft that must be coming.
Or they've enlisted, like my son, to fight
the War on Terror—pray
that friendly fire will not undo them, pray
that they will not return with nightmares featuring civilians
they have killed or buddies blasted by roadside bombs.

They usually swoop this time of year
from pecan and live oak to the chaste monk tree,
its lavender flowers waning imperceptibly
like the length
of days.
They ornament the yard
with scarlet, exploding in
the midst of all this brown and brittle life.

My mother made these birds
the theme of all her greeting cards.
She loved their flight, audacious crest and color.
Years ago she watched them from her own bride's bed.
With her new husband gone to war,
they welcomed her
to the world of summer courtship, nesting chicks.

They hardly ever failed to bring her joy.
But one day late in the summer of her year,
she stood by her door staring at the birds
and suddenly wept. Too late
to ask her now what in those scarlet streaks she saw.
A sign of loss, I guess.
Bride's blood.
A laceration on the sky.

FOR SALE BY OWNER

We know this is a murder house.
Depressed and in despair, some man
shot his wife, his son, then hanged himself.
Sold and bought four times since then,
here it is, for sale again, too much
a bargain not at least to look.

Charming Cottage. Great Starter Home.
Prime location, near good schools.
Swept clean and emptied of all signs
of life, scrubbed to glade-fresh
sterility. New carpet, paint, a fixture or two
intended to suggest that no one

ever lived here: this house can't be haunted.
With a shiver we move
to the next home on our list.
The sign on Jolly Avenue says
FOR SALE BY OWNER. We used to know
the owners, so we take the tour.

A saddle just inside the door invites us
to mount up, with a whiff of leather and horsehide.
The theme of this place is hard riding.
Cowboy art, barbed wire mounted on oak,
a rack of branding irons above
the bunkhouse stove.

It'll burn you out if you stoke it too much.

Spare rooms remain as if the kids
might come home any moment,
closets stuffed with toys for boys of every age.
We feel them growing up, moving away.
We feel them fighting. Wherever they are
they don't regret their childhood home is on the market.

No light gets in the shut up windows
of the master bedroom. Only *his* clothes hang
in the walk-in closet with the ghosts of so much anger.
He seems embarrassed by the waterbed,
its frame of heavy beams like a scaffold.
He's quick to tell us the Jacuzzi doesn't stay.

Tools and paint cans in a shed out back,
a boat for sale backed in from the alley.
The board fence is collapsing. In one corner
wrought iron encloses a small plot like a grave.
From the dirt and the dry stalks, we see
it used to be a garden.

Mudder

When the water falls enough to work, they call
us mudders in. The flood
has left its poisonous sediment of waste,
chemicals, diesel, mud,

anything disaster dredges. From a home
near the river we shovel sludge,
haul furniture, books, clothes, muck-heavy
carpet, stinking fridge.

Toss all in a pile. Strip the dry wall.
Gut it to the studs.
We lug the piano last, dreading its heft.
It breaks to pieces, wood

crack WATCH OUT! quick as a quarter note
legs collapsing, plunge
of sounding board ponderous to the floor
as a slab of Stonehenge.

Rest. Sheen and swelter. Carp plucking insects,
riverbanks broken, bend
clogged with fallen trees, roots splayed, rubbish
and wreckage. River ruined

in its own *fortissimo*. Following a few
respectful measures of silence,
we stoop to gather chop sticks. Worthless now.
Mind the splinters. This mess

of pegs and strings will never tune again.
We spot the fish amid
the warped wood, keys, and coiling wires,
snagged, mud-colored, putrid,

half petrified. It swam inside that piano
when the river rose,
trapped there as the flood receded. Caught
in the music of that house.

End of Days

She will discover your body in the app.

She will discover your beer.

She will discover intention.

In the hip that didn't work very well toward the end.

Behind the old spectacles insensible to magic.

In the pocket full of lottery tickets.

In the garden with vegetables you only pretended to like on Sundays.

On Sundays when you needed oxygen.

On Sundays cooking ribs.

On Sundays next to the lawn mower.

On Sundays thinking *Why would the Old One make woman from a piece of me brittle as a rib, hard as regret.*

Why not a thumb?

Why not a vein?

If it had to be (for the sake of metaphor) she from your side, why not from love handles or the meat of your right shoulder?

Your right thigh?

Why not asparagus?

Why not forgetfulness?

Why not forgiveness, hard as bone?

Why not need, tender as tonsils?

Why not thanks, fragile and meek?

Why make the man first? Why not his body from her body?

Why not her body from mud and his body from grass so she would know his body for once as if needing it first and last?

As if remembering every surgery.

Every planet revealed in friction.

Every intention left on the road.

Every apology lost in every crevice of marriage.

Every isthmus of wishing.

Every doubt when she looks in your dilated eyes.

Hidden in the toes of your shoes in the closet.

In a hand full of fear.

Full of phone calls.

Of procrastination.

She will discover all that was never there as you grow to her less and less in the silence.

After hyperbolic eulogies.

After the drive behind the motorcycle.

After the coffee and cookies.

When she comes to the house with no truck in the driveway.

With book shelves abandoned by books.

With unopened mail.

With the stillness of your bed.

With the still, wet sleep still ahead.

Melting

My wet black jeans steam before the cabin fire.
I think how the Wicked Witch of the West
while melting into smoky nothingness moans
an existential epithet—

whining, pathetic, incredulous.
Almost enough to make my heart ache
these days when evil has gone
into such ungraceful mutations.

> *O what a world what a world...*

Pity the old girl, whose green Semitic beak brought
a certain nasal elegance to terror, destroyed so thoroughly in all her
"beautiful wickedness" just as the ruby power
seemed within her long hook-fingered reach.

Who's going to mourn you, sister?
The Universe is laughing at your sad collapse.

What did you plan to do with all that power?
Scare insensible straw into neat cornfields?
Blast the decadent and hedonistic City
with a rub-rub here and a rub-rub there

until nothing remains but prim memorial gardens?
Did you really think a pair of shoes could make you happy,
restore pre-modern order, make all
as frigid and staid as you?

Did you think that you could stop
desire with poppies, stop
nubile girls painting their faces,
lions curling locks,

lusty tornadoes
dropping houses out of the sky
or naughty hydrogen
bonding in ménage à trois with oxygen?

All the might you craved
could not prevent the monkeys' rejoicing
or that insipid little runaway
from gaily carting off your scorched broom.

Now you're dead, the essence of your great evil
dissolved into the elements of the dream of this world,
where newborns, so to speak, suckle at your cold pap.
Dorothy is back in claptrap Kansas.

She's grown up, in fact, married a farmer
much like her Uncle Henry, as it happens—
salt-of-the-earth, baffled, spineless, always wondering
why the ends don't meet.

She's got a few kids, conceived in necessity
stronger than the smell of pig shit
that just never seems to leave the cotton sheets
or her husband's body.

Though the chickens are laying well,
Auntie Em is motionless.
Her hands have stopped wringing forever—
no more cool rags to Dorothy's head.

Pneumonia got old Zeke, cancer Hickory,
and Hunk could not outsmart dementia.
Snakebite took the precious little pooch
a few days back from Oz.

Twisters still snake across the plains
in wicked black and white,
and we always think
they are headed for the house.

Night Swimming at Sea Rim

Beneath the slow eddy of the stars,
along the gulf where oil rigs
in the distance secrete
a strange glow toward the shore,

we bathe in waters where small crabs
crawl secretly to the sand
and leave half-buried bodies for the gulls,
the keeping of some ancient promise.

Late summer. Far away on the Atlantic,
the sea spawns fury, moving in
above the gulf. Out in the swirling depths
and in these shallow continental waters,

jellyfish glide like phantoms
from our unremembered past.
And as the waves slap our thighs,
touching in the darkness,

we de-evolve, swimming back
through fetal stages of creation
to become again the first living cells
to forsake the ocean.

Some of us who stayed became
the dolphin, some the shark,
and recollections of compassion and of terror
also shape the thoughts

of those of us who left, carried
in our unconscious
as a newborn carries in her womb
the eggs of all the children she will bear.

Lovers swimming in the company of squid,
we are tossed together like sand and sea,
the spray and sky, as life and death
inseparably are joined.

Constellations brood upon us in a swirl
of mystery, a spiraling galaxy of light,
and we understand why the ancients named gods
for the miracles they feared.

Old Rabbi Dizzle to His Disciples

A dead star yanks all light
into its dead eye. Stay awake.
A teaspoon of its matter, such
a trap, heavier than whole earths
with all their density of intention.

Hell's windows glow
with just the jolliest of lights.
The fish you feast on there
flop in the stomach forever.
Anyone can make you sniff

that dish; it's up to you
to swill the foul bait down.
When done with me, cast me in
to karma's ravenous
piranha, I trust their teeth.

The jagged edges of my vices
will turn to gum by the time
my bones can reach the river's bed.
You see how bodies fall
in spite of all we say.

The sweet soul, much obliged,
remains where sweet souls
always stay. Our definitions
are mere bubbles in the churning
water where, sharp-toothed

and ever hungry, the river feeds
on every sort of chum.

Goddess Tree

She lives on the river where few men go.
The water is a living thing, winding
through forests and pastures green

with sunny light, bearing the unseen heart
of June. I tie to a root and step ashore
to picnic in her summer shade,

a canopy of creamy blooms.
I spread my blanket on the ground.
I spread elder jelly on a slice of bread.

Mystical elder. The softest solid on earth
is the pith of her new growth. Her heartwood
white and hard as polished moon.

Wand wood, rood wood,
she bears the body of hope in death.
Drowsy and dreamy in the heat of noon,

I listen and hum the hymn of her leaves
under the limb where the traitor hangs.
She kisses away every note of my grief.

All the lazy afternoon until night comes,
I sit in her serene benevolence
singing and sipping her elegant wine.

The Triple Goddess

Song of the Goddess of Gladness

When the beautiful lady
walks in the garden,
all flowers turn toward her.
In the midst of sunny meadow,
in orchards of summer shadow,
pistil and petal, stem and stamen—
conception without reservation.

Why would a leaf question the light?
Her smile is the seed of greenness.
Every enchantment ripens
as she sings the bounty of being.
In the midst of rainy ruin,
in winter dungeons of creation,
wherever she is becomes Eden.

Five

The fifth of May will arrive in the fifth May
after the gray flint of the bare-limb dream
of graves. There will be rain in some hollow
and frost will still walk on the leaves some nights.
A ladder will lean into a tree leading
from obituaries to blossoms. Abandoned tracks
like inspiration will wish for a beggar,
and in the Red Rooster, where the billiard balls
crash and pop on the green like drunken particles
of wrong and right, a bum will hear the wish,
grow sad, and say *there's no way to reach
the white lady by parallel lines forget it
I'm just a drunk it's all in my mind.*
In the city of mystical bruises a streetlight
will turn green a second too late. Meanwhile,
down a country lane, a girl with a faux fur
boa will sneak out of her house to meet
whoever is waiting—a fifth son—behind
the glow of a cigarette with a thrill in his feet
and the same on his mind. May will slip off
a glove to touch the face of the girl, and she
will learn the myth of herself for the first time.
Under the elder that shades them from moonlight,
a pantheon of goddesses will come alive.

The Giant Who Had No Heart in His Body

Kitty, kitty asleep on the rug beside the fire,
queen with your green Egyptian eyes,
the wind's in the window, ice on the plough.
For you I strum my well-tuned chords.
Impetuoso, appassionato,
for you I play this hollow instrument.
So what if my heart is under the door?
You have what is yours, you have me now.
Why wish to hold a giant's heart?
Just love me in your mammal joy
and take my mammal voice.

Pussy, puss pacing and mewing underfoot,
queen of this mountain with animal shins,
the wind's in the window, ice on the plough.
I offer you cream and food in cans.
I give you fresh water and a toy on a string.
I split wood for the fire to keep away chill.
So what if my heart is on the shelf?
You have what is yours, you have me now.
Why wish to hold a giant's heart?
Just love me in your mammal way
and take my mammal day.

Cat, cat shredding my clothes and couch,
queen scratching my thighs with feline claws,
the wind's in the window, ice on the plough.
I twirl my thumbs around your ears,
I stroke your flanks and sweetly whisper
as you purr and weave your tail in the air.
So what if my heart is in the well?
You have what is yours, you have me still.
Why wish to own a giant's heart?
Just love me in your mammal pride
and take my mammal night.

Drop

after the painting *Pagoda in Rain at Dusk*
by Kasamatsu Shiro

When I ponder the prayers of raindrops,
lady, I picture you far away within
the shelter of some eastern pagoda.
Neither sun nor shade can thirst as we
of finial, eave, and gutter, we fallen
droplets, forbidden to touch your face.

Light can crawl through windows to caress you,
shadows creep from corners for a kiss.

But we rain people, dragon-like, must call
on all our cunning, seek the loose
or broken shingle, follow gravity and pitch
along the clever trusses down the intricate
architecture of your house to reach
through so many stories your bashful glory.

The Nudes of Flaunteur

Absorbed in those enthralling nudes of Flaunteur
I remember the body is mostly water.
Every cell has a healthy regard for matter,
a wholesome respect for the metaphysical power

of evaporation. Particles pop in and out
of existence so often it's impossible to know
with any assurance that we ever
actually hold more than once the same lover.

Consider his *Alayna Eau.*
The curves of her figure flow
in linear solidity, her hair cascades in tangled rivulets,
her breasts (of course) drift in silky currents.

Yet all her flesh is but a little seed of matter,
her beauty insubstantial as magnetics—even her strange
white lips (a Flaunteur trademark), elfishly parted,
eager to whisper to me alone the secrets of her atoms.

Goodwill of Southern California

At first I thought it was only a shoe,
unmatched and scuffed among one
and a thousand pristine pairs
in the closet behind the bedroom
where the starlet overdosed. Airless
as a vault that walk-in was,
and wide as Walmart, but lighted
by only a single naked bulb, strung
on white electrical wire.

When I saw what it was, of course
I rubbed.
       A raw red tendon of greasy smoke—
the gritty crush of bones—tissues
twisting—skin stretching—the reek
of burning hair and meat—a scream
as the body of the genie undissolved
from the shot of melted atoms in the lamp—
and last of all in a swirl of guts
the abdomen filled and the giant—stuffed—hung
by a wisp of bloody umbilicus.

It broke from the spout, gross
as an addict gone to fat, and all
you could look at in that hall
of spiked heels, leather soles, and straps
was that blistered belly, black-veined and hairy,
with its smug navel, like puckered lips
blowing a final circle of smoke,
urging you to wish.

Flannery's Peacocks

She never felt the urgent pressure of
another body, peacock light
of need simple as livestock that live
to graze and scratch at grain or pellets
digestible as truth that never germinates.

Virginity never knew that barnyard business,
cock and hen, peabirds
so reluctant to spread their tails she'd come to doubt
those bright eyes even exist.
Strut and shriek, snake-eating, earth-bound, weak fliers.

She learned a grace that never shows
its glory on command. Only by
surprise, bursting unexpected in brilliant defense
of color, gaudy invitation.
Her ill and clumsy body stirred

to their brilliant, shimmering, erectile
iridescence. And she,
the keeper of birds, never tired
of their showy revelation
peeping through eyes of vainglorious feathers.

Nearest Neighbors

Red light seeps from the windows
of the house next door—the room
in back, nearest my fence. Red light
wetting the waiting trees with juice.
Grandmother, mother, teen.
The mom's ex helped them move in.
I helped him lug in the new frig.
No sign of him since.

Early and late, I hear their fighting
and grief. The mom is icon of anger.
The crone is image of brood. The girl
has a scar on her knee and a spell
on the back of her shorts. Their dog
cries at night, so I offer her little hearts
through a slit in the boards while the red
light gushes out of the windows.

The light might be made by a red shade
or a scarlet cloth draped over the lamp.
Perhaps a red bulb screwed in the socket
for psychedelic effect, inferno or disco.
Or could it be the flood of their rage?
Or the fierce radiance of their guardian
angels squeezed out of the house
for the night to catch?

Satchel Full of Women's Faces

Into a satchel he pours their faces,
wildly, meekly mortified.
And some are witches, some are graces.

Nymphs and nuns, devout and aspish,
mount on barges side by side.
Into a satchel he pours their faces.

Beaten screamless by their rapists
daughters, mothers opened wide.
And some are witches, some are graces.

Fanny in flames upon a stake is
extorting needles from her hide.
Into a satchel he pours their faces.

Kill your husband, tear the laces
from your corset, virgin bride.
And some are witches, some are graces.

They lure him in to holy places
deep within the black cowhide.
Into a satchel he pours their faces,
and some are witches, some are graces.

Sayeth the Preacher

Let the widows not chatter in church.
Let them not whisper in pews
across places they leave for dead husbands.
Let them not arrange their long afternoons.

(*Who will bring the deviled eggs?*
Will it be Bridge or Bunco?) Let them
not fret at the sight of the widower's hair.
(*Poor man, why does nobody tell him?*)

They must not dispute, when the Prelude begins,
the shade of vestments, the choice of hymns.
For the sake of our precious devotion, let ladies
be still in the church and tranquil as tombs.

By no means do we need commentary
on who carries the chalice, who frowns at the Peace.
Blather of grandkids cuts order to pieces,
Gossip of nieces kills gravitas.

If even Lord Jesus, formed out of wood,
comes down from His high tree still wounded,
to the cross of their mouths let them nail their tongues.
The Ghost will not be offended.

Let only the men who are raised up to speak
have a voice at the service. That all may be decent
and sweet in God's house,
let the women be silent.

Apheresis

I'm not into karma, accountability, keeping score,
matching good deeds against my sins
(venal/mortal, omission/commission),
still I donate blood as often as
the UBS will let me—

      THREE TEASPOONS CAN
      SAVE A BABY'S LIFE

gallons over the years, a bunch
of brats at half an ounce a life.

For years I gave whole blood. Then
platelets for a while, but it took all afternoon,
so these days it's double reds.
For the squeamish let me say there's little pain.
The worst of it is all the questions.
How many times must I assure this girl?
> *I never traded money for sex   had sex*
> *with anyone who has   am not*
> *giving blood to test for AIDS*
> *haven't taken aspirin in the past three days*
> *am feeling well enough right now.*

Inflating her cuff on my humerus,
she rubs the skin in the crook of my arm,
admires the purple plumpness of the vein.
Warning me to look away she slides
the needle in with vascular ease,
the slightest sting, then cranks up the machine
that sorts my blood, offers bedding
(blanket, pillow) and a smile.

I squeeze a rubber heart or brain.
I hear the machine at work,
sorting the blood. Plasma and saline

return to the vein, cool as a daiquiri.
I close my eyes—squeezing squeezing—
sensing the life going from me
("forgive us our trespasses")
to some other body.

I like to observe my sweet phlebotomist.
She calls me "Mister" and "Sir"
but flirts with wiccan confidence
as she floats about the room, alert,
nice shape, nice face, serving us who bleed,
blessing me with her wild green eyes.

The ancients believed that life is in the blood.
They conjured ghosts with it
and gave it to their students to drink with bread.
The earth absorbs the spillage, numberless wounds,
injuries and disease inflicted on
the tender human tissue.
                           Pondering
the softness of all mortal flesh
as she pulls the needle out, I fantasize
about this brave and lovely goddess,
with all her unappreciated power,
which I alone can see.
Bewitched by her, I dream
that we are white blood cells, streaming
together at lightning speed through all the dark
arteries of the world
to save it.

Old Aunt Helen's Ode to Passion

Passion tosses and turns
on a pile of folded clothes.

Timid, alarmed by body noises
and good order:
stomach rumblings, the slightest
cough, Commandments, calendars
with every Thursday marked at 3.

A delicate fish
it darts to the sound of streams.
The current always runs ahead.

     i look best in candlelight

Lips wet with the meat of fresh ripe figs.
Pop of a cork, glasses touching.
Passion wants to see
its own reflection wished
in the eyes of cufflinks.

Two blades
so in love whatever comes between
gets cut.

     i bleed at the slightest treason

Used edges grow dull.
Disappointment bruises.
The mundane meal opens a vein.
     cut my heart out
     feed it to thanks
     you would not treat a unicorn so
     pick up your clothes
     put the seat down please
     someone is listening

how could you forget it was on the list
don't answer the phone i said don't answer
where's my other stocking
where's my diaphragm
you forgot the rubbers

Passion travels abroad,
prefers sea air, settles down
with blacksmiths.

Passion sleeps it off
through holidays,
through gossip and dementia.

Passion never warns with a bell.
Passion finishes with a gong,
leaves fluids and stains.

i am looking for some new abode
of bashfulness where
your clumsy tongue will not injure silence
where your icy hands will not scrawl in red
helter-skelter *on the walls*

Retiring to the Tropics

She is my one to "notify in case
of emergency." When she walks with me
along the foamy margin of the sea
I feel all my disgrace ebbing in her grace.
Without any kind of magic I raise her house
with clumsy tools—hammer, handsaw, brace
and bit, level, plane—sweating crude boards
from densely unpopulated offshore woods.
Spark to fire in the mud hearth. In the spell
of salty dawns and driftwood windy eaves
our cauldron boils. When she is old
I feed her puddings. We are castaways
discovering a lost Atlantis as we stroll
between the shady forest and the waves.

Rabbi Dizzle Visits Old Aunt Helen
at the Home

A bedside tray.
A carton red and white of tepid milk.
From dentureless dementia she stirs
and speaks to me
of certain boys who suckled.
                    whose are these?

Her plate at lunch,
two tomato slices—
the red wheels of her bike, wrecked
one day in the neighbor's garden.
                    momma washed my bleeding face

A girl who slept beside her once
                    pajama party popcorn root beer we
                    painted one another's fingernails toenails
                    she touched my breast
touched her breast, thinking her asleep,
the others sleeping, breathed
upon her neck. The house so quiet
she dared not move.
                    she had my mother's name

Ripe red fruit
smashed against dry soil.
                    their red gums bit my nipples
                    i pretended to be asleep
Tomatoes broke from the vine,
one wheel of her bike kept spinning.
                    my thigh was bleeding

All those years she carried longing
in her wallet like coins in a secret pocket.
                    i wish i could go back to that party
                    be touched again
                    with that girl's touch

The smell of her pretty hair
               nothing like the way these old crones smell
now as far from her reach as Cassiopeia.

Wishing
for a magic wand
or a time machine
or a genie's wish
               their red gums bit my nipples
               momma washed my face and thigh
all her life she pacified her need
               boys made from bones
               inside me
               boys I cradled in my arms
               boys with their eager mouths
               always on me
in the usual way.
               i never forgot how that girl breathed
               in the bed beside me
               when she finally fell asleep

In the Closet

after cremation
her blue sari

Berries and Brambles

Plums: A Fairy Tale

> I have eaten the plums
> —William Carlos Williams

Aloysius picks plums on a sunny day.
That sentence is delicious, and if I had my wishes
I would be with Aloysius picking plums
from the plum tree on a sunny day.

Once this wish occurs to me, curiously
I begin to dream of plums repetitiously,
of a sunny plum grove, populous
with plums obsessively delicious,

and in it Aloysius. The more I ponder Aloysius
the more it seems I absolutely must,
must taste those plums he's picking.
That is all my wishing.

My head is of a knotty thickness,
and I am superstitiously suspicious,
so as the elder is my witness
I'll shake the bushes for my wishes.

> *I'll travel over hill,*
> *I'll journey down the dale,*
> *I'll sweat and pant in sun,*
> *I'll shiver in the hail,*
> *I'll cross the rickety bridges,*
> *I'll trudge through muddy ditches,*
> *I'll ask the way of strangers,*
> *I'll skip amid the dangers.*

I'll leave, if leave I must,
the world I know
and to some nether world
will gladly go.

You may no longer think me sane
when I turn down that lane
toward the grove where grow
the plums, but I—I seriously won't mind
as long as I can find
                                    my way
to Aloysius picking plums delicious
from the plum tree on a sunny day.

Spring

copperhead strikes my boot
new moon spills a milky drop
on the elder tree

Air Guitar

Bare-assed in rain, we hooted and sang,
banging axes conjured from the vapors
of Kentucky Tavern. Screaming rock stars

deep in the woods, our cheeky lyrics
and riotous chords reached high Heaven.
Riding on wisps of cumulus, ghostly groupies

juked and shrieked, wild for the oracle
of sudoric voices. Numinous remains
of ethicists, aroused, applauded in brazen joy

the purity of sharps and flats
which snubbed all arguments of despair.
Talent scouts and record execs, unexpectedly

ascended, wept to consider the piles
of dough they might have made
on the leaven of our mad and happy riffs.

Meanwhile, the hardpan road, our stage,
rolled on and on through hills
to our moonshine fame.

At the end of our set, the high, green pines,
our gods, rocked on, rain fingering the frets
of their stoic, glistening boughs.

monk's chaste tree

monks brewed the berries
to keep their
vows

vestal virgins carried twigs
for cold and patient
Demeter

"menopause made easy"
"my husband's favorite
herb"

perfume of June promiscuous
with birds and
blossoms

The Wild Blackberries

According to their custom,
blackberries shelter copperheads.
A field mouse is the thorn's familiar.
Spiders hover among the leaves,
home to tick and chigger,
moth and ladybug.

According to my custom,
on Midsummer Day I go berry picking.
More than a year's weather
meets me in the meadow
where moon and stars engorge
the night-stained fruit.

All of us know our habits here,
down to the loamy soil.
Sun and rain have reconciled
in an aggregate of succulence,
ripe and whole.
The sweetness paints my fingertips.

Happy Hour

Twin sisters on a swing
push little bare feet
toward the green velvet music
of the elder limbs.

Two green-striped lizards
prance from the woodpile
to dance like fairies
in a circle of shade.

Tomatoes ripen
on lush green vines
that swirl in their cages
leafy letters of thanks.

Blue jay, mocker, cardinal, dove—
tipsy beaks in the birdbath.
Owl in the elder
below a sliver of moon.

The Pears

These pears remember the last wish
of Socrates. Imperfectly green,
sun-splotched, bruised from their falling.
Sweeter than certainty.
Stone bowl. Stone table. Windowless stone
house under the white stone moon.
This fruit will not explode
stone Buddhas, burn houses, give
poison, make
speeches for war in the agora.
Rest and ripen.
Stem, peel, pulp, seed, and root.
Luscious with the flavor
of all they do not know.

Risking Life and Limb
for the Fruits of the Season,
Rabbi Dizzle Ponders Kinetics

Photon function. Fractal flow.
Rabbi Dizzle ambulates among
impatient cars and trucks. Fenders,
feathers, beak, claw, shadow, shell,
all he sees. Blissful grackles peck
and pick tire-crushed fragments
of fractured pecans. Black tread
marks in the shape of risk.
A nervous mastiff, tall as a man
(pyramid snout and galaxy tongue)
warns Rabbi Dizzle from inside a fence.
Wind and leaf, golden grass,
golden glow where steeples rise
above the feckless passersby.
Rabbi Dizzle looks both ways,
steps off the curb and into the road.
He dodges Dodges, Chevys, Fords.
Grills and wheels and squealing brakes.
Ever mindful of motion and mass,
he tips his vegetarian hat to one
indignant motorist and steps
out of the street, back on the curb.
He chooses two unblemished nuts.
Giving thanks, he makes a fist.
Newtonian miracle of muscle
and nerve shatters the pecans.
When he opens his hand, behold!
Jagged fractals of broken shell.
Fat fragments of meaty fruit.

Fall

first frost—
icy vines
with one red tomato

Pyre

for Karl Kopp

With sadness we
announce...

So Death surprises me
from a thousand miles
and thirty years away—
the old teacher
I lost touch with.

His obituary
brings the smoke
of an old chimney
filling October.
Green brier, grape leaves.
Homebrew and elderberry wine
on the weathered porch
of his mountain shack.
Poetry at the hearth
of the goddess.
Midnight laughter,
down comforters
over pallets on the floor,
the jovial fire
lighting the way
to lush, dreamless, decadent sleep.

I wonder how
I had forgotten that.
How could I have lived
without it?

Now half my life
since I saw him last,
the pyracantha drips

with rain in my own
backyard. I marvel
how this ancient,
unexpected grief
rekindles all that joy.

Teamind

In the garden of infinite beauty,
as spring water heats in a green kettle
on my charcoal brazier, a fly
alights upon my humble mat.
Map-winged with dung-muddy legs,
she anticipates the tea so carefully brewed.

Death-feather, born of corpses, gift
of vision, I do not ask instead of you
for eagle, raven, crow, or white
androgynous angel of revelation.
Every nation is a facet of your eyes.
I hear the words of your watching,

eloquence of piercing mandible.
None can sing such delicate strokes
on the scroll of meditation. O highest guest
of all that is, sip from my best bowl,
hallowed above all birds
in the ceremony of my serving.

Source of Light

Some people think they need to explain
everything. Changing the locks and why
the dog carried off a particular
shoe. Even the ground that ministers
to insects. The ice cream just not
quite sweet enough. Why someone
left or someone didn't. Why Q follows P
in the Alphabet. Just sit
beside me here, listen and watch
while I don't explain my arm
around you, the rain outside
or the fire in here, how the wood
cheerfully gives itself to heat the house,
how the angles of every shadow
track to a single point
if only we follow them far enough.

Mild Mid-Winter Evening: A Visitation

After a housebound week of cold
we share a bottle of wine on our patio.
Inside, our empty house
is still.

A rustling in the live oak
where we saw the owl
attracts the notice of a pair of doves
basking on the highest wire.

Your perennials are draped with cloth.
The grass is brown.
All our summer vegetation
decomposes in the compost pile.

Passing through our wine
the setting sun casts crimson angels
on the plastic tabletop. Sip by sip,
as night draws in, we drink them up.

Reptilian

Raking mulch to plant
my pansies, I disturb
a dormant horny toad asleep
at the feet of St. Francis.

She sprints a few paces
from my iron rake and comes
to a leaden stop.
Presumably, I've killed her.

Poor thing,
how will I make amends
to our Sister Mother Earth?
In agony I kneel

to look for trauma, dreading
to see what I assume I'll see
on the fresh-turned dirt—
Sister Bodily Death, so rarely welcome.

I resign to give myself to praise
and Sister Lizard to the ground:
Blessed is she whom Death will find
in holy will. Amen.

Then reaching
with my gloved hand, I see
her sides heaving
with the air of late winter.

O Brother Sun!
she stares ahead, unwounded,
still but quick,
warming her lazy blood in your light!

Ripening

How will I ripen
here in these deep last days?
How will I finally reach the sea?

Like a boat
with some bearded, battered,
storm-bitter captain battling every wave
to stay afloat?

Like a tuber rotting in the ground,
which never knew the morning moon?

No.

I will be
a mountain stream
that has tumbled
down
       cliffs
       gushing
       rushing
           crash and roar
brimming with the summer melt of glaciers
churning
       through chasms and canyons
                     to a wider flow.

I will be
a nut near the nest of a crow.
I have seen the hatchlings hatch and grow,
I have urged them all to spread their wings.

Having taken the sun through summer and spring,
when autumn bathes me
in a sea-borne wind, I can simply
                     let

                    go.

The Thirteenth Moon

Flowers for Li Bai

Li Bai concocts a silver alchemy.
Li Bai climbs cliffs with a jug for his spree.
Li Bai inquires what key shall I play.
Steep the path and bright the way.

Li Bai stirs potions making Li Bai strong.
Li Bai sings sky through Li Bai's lung.
Drunk in the morning, high all alone,
Li Bai draws friends in the chattering dawn.

Li Bai dies. The soft, falling snow
Fills Li Bai's dreams with tracks of the crow.
Li Bai comes down with hoot and shout,
Li Bai blossoming within, without.

Empire of the Body

Our empire is small, only a body.
Yet We are no small tyrant, subject to
unscrupulous ambition, anointed to reign
in icy discontent with gracelessness
and narcissistic malice sourly blaming
Our body for its dimensions, its
poverty and unimportance. Nor do
We claim or covet any parts apart
from Our domains, though freely We confess
in the sometime loneliness of Our
imperial isolation a rare and wonton wish
to annex or otherwise enlarge Our boundaries,
if even by surrender, perhaps becoming
jointress with some benign and willing neighbor.

Let Us meantime avow benevolent
despotism, unfettered by the rule
of multitudes—each citizen a theory to
himself, and partisan of her own pleasure.
Our state is not less delicate than a premise,
yet such is Our fatherly affection
that in Our eyes it is perfect
for its little imperfections—its interest
in strong drink, its wounds susceptible
to infections, its feet to fungus.

One would think We need not fear invasion
for Our frontiers are itchy with some chronic
eczema, and none would call Our capital
beautiful.
              Yet many have launched
against Our towers, and without
a standing army, We govern in
perpetual dis-easiness of defense.

Loving monarch, enlightened despot that

We are, We could not cherish Our body more
than the whole of lovely France with all its sunny
vineyards, more than constellations, galaxies,
with who knows what kings to rule them
in their ever-shifting darkness. Tenderly
We cherish all Our subjects—all—
enduring all their clamorous supplications,
listing to their cacophonous songs at court,
applauding every joint and member
with genuine approval and affection.

Yet We fear. States exist
in a confusion of power, and We
are meager and heirless
as all emperors are.
We know that even now for all Our love
and against their good Our so-called
loyal subjects are plotting revolution—
the block, the gallows, or the guillotine.
We only pray (since kingdoms rise and fall
by proverbial inevitability)
that a certain steadiness, a ready
and unselfish peace, empowers Us
to at the very least avert, in the chaos
of sedition, the loss of Our own passion
to trivial cruelty or indifference,
that We, its heart and will, will love Our empire
to the end having suffered no evil in
Ourselves and no corruption so We may bear
it boldly to the earth, that realm that is forever.

Young and Old

No doubt millions have groaned and rightly so
to learn the average Elizabethan baby
got a fresh diaper only every four days.

Wet rags hung above the fire
with kettle and the roasting goose.
Times have changed,

somewhat. A TV show I sometimes watch
extols the invention of the disposable diaper,
a "Modern Marvel."

A man would never have thought of such a thing
in those days when for a man to change
a diaper was as rare

as a sex change or divorce or sex in the park.
Now the genius of disposable diapers is obvious
to all but environmentalists,

the greatest thing since Kinsey and Jane Roe
despite the heaps of non-biodegradable refuse
piled every day higher than the Pyramid of Khufu.

I too concede the brilliance of Marion Donovan's device.
But I had a mystic experience once while
washing cloth diapers. My first child,

a daughter, wore cotton nappies (poverty
compelled us, not social conscience)
and went through 10 or 12 a day. One night

in the apartment Laundromat, up to my elbows
in water, diapers, sour curds, and Borax,
I saw my old English teacher, Francis,

who had recently died. He stood and watched me a while then
murmured an incantation straight from the ether:
"I used to do that, too."
                              The cosmos

erupted into beauty, unity, and purpose
and a brilliant Wordsworthian moon shone on the moment
until I wrung the rinse water from the last

pure white all cotton diaper in my pail.
I think that proves you sometimes have to plunge
your hands in shit to effect a revelation.

Francis was blessed. He choked
on a chunk of rib-eye or just might be alive today,
wearing Depends, like the men in the commercials

who want to golf, take road trips, go fishing
but are bound to the house
because their organs

keep them searching out rest stops,
constantly prowling for the nearest head, oblivious
as Elizabethan newborns to the thrill of a kiss in the park.

Introspect of Retrospect: An Intimation

> Go in fear of abstractions.
> —Ezra Pound

At last I am awake
enough to say
that my "best smith" was full
of himself, and the dear good doctor,
pillar of my temple,
got it only half-way right.

Why should he not?
William, if you spend your life
in stubborn joy
fingering rectums, delivering babies,
surely you are bound to intimate at least
what's underneath all that.

I think you saw it, too, Ezra,
the face behind those faces in the crowd,
but wouldn't trust the eye of your eyes.
Abstractions are more real
than cats or plums or broken glass.
Rejoice, old hens. Keep warm

until dawn comes. Truth is a perfect sun
inside every imbecile,
and Beauty is the beam of every atom.
Yes. Even in the flesh of fanatics.
Even in the skin
of every murdering Mussolini.

Art

The boy is mopping McDonald's.
An easy delight—don't miss a spot.
Jolly as a brand new coloring book.
I lift my feet, I'm in the way.
Nah, you're not.
He moves that mop as though creating art.

Who says he's not?
Ball cap, spectacles, double-X shirt coming untucked,
he spills art from his blue bucket.
Art from his narrow shoulders and bespectacled mind.

I admire his work.
His way of working is art to me.
What if I call him "Art"?

Art swipes his mop across the floor in graceful strokes.
I lift my feet so Art can mop beneath my table;
Art smiles, pleased with my attention.
Art is Thank-You beautiful, slender and ageless.
I suddenly love Art more than TV.
Art makes me glad as heat on a cold day,
joy like the steam rising from his bucket.
Art makes me live to know his unaffected competence.
Art excites me more than suicide.
Art is wiser than war.
Art never broke a promise.
Art fills the trenches neater than the junk we throw away.
Art mocks the dignity of tsunamis.
Art wipes my spirit clean, starts the day over again,
shows me that in setting out I have already arrived.

Art's strokes evaporate on the floor.
But I remember the nimble caress,
the easy arc of his mop across the brown tile,
and that makes me the rich collector of his genius.

The Art of Seeing
Revealed in the Diagnosis
of Approaching Blindness

When they tell you that you will soon be blind,
you see
how blind you have always been.
Doves and finches materialize
in the blue evening.
A corona of sunlight
embracing the moon's body
makes that gray stone a goddess again.
Some childhood scar, faintest scallop
on your lover's throat—
could that have been there
all these years?

Gazing into the eyes of your child,
who wasn't even there
the last time you didn't even look,
you fall right through the iris,
into light so deep
that only now your night can comprehend.
You who will soon see nothing now see,
like letters on a page, beams that have sped light years
to teach you the art of vision,
to bless you with the boon of all you never knew you saw,
are seeing now,
will never see.

The Party behind One Eye

When the surgeon puts my eye back in he gets it backward so I get a peek back there and see a teen-aged boy in feathered Alpine hat taking long strides and soaking up the view.

He sees the boundless blue well of the sky.

He sees the mountain forests all ablaze with light.

He sees a venerable Chinaman with paper, a brush, and a pot of ink headed who knows where.

He sees a red-bearded baseball coach, lotus of the diamond, serenely meditating in a blue tutu.

He sees a pudgy grizzly bear with glasses sashaying and pirouetting in summer rain.

He sees a young Queen exotically dancing with lots of loot in garters and G-string.

He sees a weather-beaten shepherd with three fingers of sheep strumming antique guitar with scars accompanied on bongos by happy Bob Marley with his fabled dreadlocks.

He sees a smiling Michael Brown playing Go Fish with Inspector Clouseau.

He sees a lovely drag queen decorating her face with cockedelic pencil powder paint.

He sees, tattooed, a Goth girl with an elder wand painting zebras sunflowers angels wedges of cheese.

He sees Bert Lahr in full lion regalia wistfully inspecting a tethered lamb and having a cool drink of bourbon with the Witch of the West.

He sees Apuleius having coffee and bagels with Jesus the Christ.

He sees Anwar Sadat and Menachem Begin baking cookies with Mary Baker Eddy for a very sweet, very old Ethiopian lady in lingerie so sexy it makes my very eyelids twitch.

Seeing him see all that I say to them all *hi ya'll.*

The boy with the Alpine hat says *hi* right back.

And everyone else says *hi welcome to the party behind your eye.*

I begin to say *wow this is quite a—*

But that's just when the surgeon must have figured out he had my eye in outside in and inside out.

He pops it out and turns it back around.

Alas, I could no longer see the revelry behind my eye.

I hear the surgeon say *oh now it's right again.*

I try to tell him *no you got it wrong* but apparently I'm still asleep.

When they wake me up I'm stuck looking out at a world I hardly recognize.

Therefore these days I doff an Alpine hat and wear it as I walk making friends with everyone and everything I see.

I smile to think that if I saw all that behind one eye I can hardly wait to see what I'll see when I see behind the other.

Mirror in a Box

Inside a box of elder wood
I look to find a mirror made
of moon. Peeping back from there
at me I see a hollow stare.
I shut the lid to keep it there.
Because I hate that face of shame
I hide it under all my rhymes,
vulgar ditties, graceless hymns,
lyrics both profane and holy
composed for gods of gore and glory.
To burn the incest of my lyre,
I hang my silver tree with fire
and put it in. I put in all
I ever did for good or ill.
Bodies hallowed, bodies hurt,
snakes of blessing, birds of curse,
the east and west of love and hate,
the north and south of will and fate—
all this stuff I stuff inside
the box made out of elder wood.
I hide my evil with my good
so when the dark of winter dawns
I will not see my shame in the moon.
But when the winter stars arrive
the box bursts open like a hive.
Lo! not a thing remains inside
the box made out of elder wood.
I look in the mirror moon within.
The face I thought was there is gone.

Yaw

My final embarkation has arrived.
I drift in the harbor of a red evening
recalling all my odyssey.

I might have shouted orders
to stalwart men below the mast,
chased mermaids in mists,
plucked Nereids below the wave-lifted keel,
fought hydras in a foam-toothed vortex.
I might have sailed in a foolish season,
tempting death in the fury of
some god's angry trident, to come at last
to a calm port, famous
and treasure-laden.

Well. My compass did not point
toward such exploits. Let the Sirens
sing in vain their fatal solicitations.
Let every Kraken I might have slain
survive to haunt and hamper
the sleek swift ships of other heroes.
I navigated other gusts and currents.

My stars aligned for a fate
of unexpected duty. I set my sail
in the wind of an ordinary god.
I seized—piss ant, pollywog—the wheel
of a different voyage, hauled my life in,
hand over hand, stood dogwatch
as the vessel yawed westward
and the long boats rowed out of range.

I became myself in Circe's spell
and sang in the burden of her giving
as she kissed the elder.

                    If I sailed
with less than the sea's whole heart,
with less than a captain's resolve and joy,
let my body go down to monsters of the dark,
let my ship founder in the wake
of dissolving stars.

The Science

Slugs weave a sticky pattern on the floor.
Roaches and rodents ooze out of the baseboards
to look for little leavings of desire.
How can I clear this room
to create a house where every appetite,
every battle and death
lead to beauty?

I know what I must know.
Slugs dissolve in the salt of a single word.
The roaches scatter in light.
Finally I lift my gaze to the blue brightness
where I see only what is real.

In the pure air of that temple,
those distracting vermin
are simply no longer there

and never were.

Unity

I have given all my clothes away
and offered the offerings
I brought with me—
my linens, my weapons,
my familiar grains—and thus

I have broken
all bonds with time
and become a leaf of the earth.
Freed from language
and ties of blood,

from altar and banner unbound,
I find there are those
who acknowledge me kin,
formed like me
of the very first light.

We slip away
from our little lands
on gusts of sullen heat and raging cold,
through biting pestilence of weevil and worm,
bound for the high place of storm and fire.

With age upon age
of leaves we flow as one
into the boundless breath of night,
into the black beatitude,
into the ether of wordless joy.

Postcard from Mars

Li Bai is gone
to polar ice
to pick blossoms
from Silver River.
                    Alone
in the Labyrinth of Night
I share his wine
with two moons.

The Guest of Spring

My springtime guest at last has come
to be the hostess of my winter home.

On a stretch of stream, water thrills
its stony bed. The sea beguiles
the sand of every beach
as far as highest tide can reach.

The one who came as my spring guest
learned all that I hid in cupboard and chest,
in every cellar drawer and attic box,
in every purpose and paradox.

Horizon and hunter's eye
are wave and coast.
Songbird and summer sky
are haven and host.

In the very wild nights when the moon was young
bonny companions joined in dance and song.
Their eyes and their tongues spilled and filled
every mansion of me, but still
there was a door and a room and a desk
for my spring guest.

In her wise eager way my guest declared,
Beauty blooms before the blossom sets.
Love lives best in winter's rarest air.
Spring is nearest neighbor of Death.

In a leather book (I know where it is)
I copied the words of my peerless guest
as she slept in my house
in the spring.

In spring,
violet and daffodil,
dogwood and jonquil
blow in every breath,
and on a mossy green hill
the springtime rain lets fall
a sweet first kiss.

Now in the night by her fountain of fire,
I settle myself without desire
on her plushest couch beneath a green
velvet throw. I listen and rest
as my hostess of winter in her voice of spring
recites sweet rhymes to her welcome guest.

Crone

A minute to midnight now,
far from the lovely hour
of labor and wild joy.
There's little to say of the man I was.
I emptied all my strength
and nerve in hallowed work,
and all who cut the elder tree

can see I bear the marks in me.
I knelt in the death of every day
to breathe the beauty
of glad desire. So I come
to this night with no regret.
Here in the icy hour of my year
I pour for the one who guards the door

to the dark of the inner realm
my white pith, fountain
of gushing gratitude—for living roots
fast in earth, for moon-bright blossoms,
for sun-soaked leaves
on every limb that shaded my way,
for vintages of healing fruit,

and above all else for the Mother Crone,
who formed me
in the fragrance of her green intent
and sang to me in storm and war
then called me to a sunny road
and bore me
home.

www.ingramcontent.com/pod-product-compliance
Lightning Source LLC
Chambersburg PA
CBHW031140090426
42738CB00008B/1160